About Skill Builders Grammar

by Isabelle McCoy, M.Ed. and Leland Graham, Ph.D.

Welcome to RBP Books' Skill Builders series. Like our Summer Bridge Activities collection, the Skill Builders series is designed to make learning both fun and rewarding.

Based on NCTE (National Council of Teachers of English) standards and core curriculum, this grade 3 workbook uses a variety of fun and challenging exercises to teach and reinforce basic grammar concepts. Exercises are grade appropriate, teacher created, and classroom tested, with clear directions and examples to introduce new concepts. As students complete the exercises and games, they will learn about parts of speech, verb tense, subject-verb agreement, sentence types, capitalization, punctuation, contractions, and words such as antonyms and synonyms that often give students trouble.

A creative thinking skills section lets students have some fun with language while testing out their new knowledge.

Learning is more effective when approached with an element of fun and enthusiasm—just as most children approach life. That's why the Skill Builders combine entertaining and academically sound exercises with eye-catching graphics and fun themes—to make reviewing basic skills at school or home fun and effective, for both you and your budding scholars.

www.summerbridgeactivities.com

Table of Contents

What are nouns?

A **noun** is a word that names a person, place, or thing.

Example:

person	Betty
place	Chicago
thing	book

Directions: Read the following sentences, and circle all of the **nouns**. The number in parentheses at the end of the sentence tells how many nouns are in the sentence.

1. Raccoons are animals that usually come out at night. (3)
2. In North America, there are 25 kinds of raccoons. (3)
3. A raccoon usually weighs 12–16 pounds. (2)
4. The raccoon usually has four to ten dark rings on its tail and a black mask across its face. (5)
5. Raccoons like swampy areas or woods near water. (4)
6. Their favorite foods are frogs, fish, and acorns. (4)
7. They usually hunt for food at night and stay in their dens during the day. (4)
8. Raccoons that live in wooded areas have their dens in a hollow log, stump, or tree. (6)
9. The colonists caught raccoons and made their pelts into caps, overcoats, and robes. (6)

Common Nouns

Nouns that name any person, place, or thing are called **common nouns**.

Example: boy, mice, body, city, school, raccoon
The **raccoon** chased the **mice**.

Directions: Underline the common nouns.

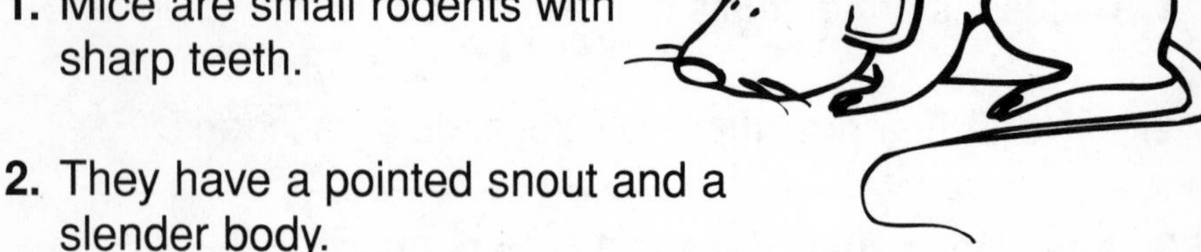

1. Mice are small rodents with sharp teeth.
2. They have a pointed snout and a slender body.
3. Harvest mice live in grassy or marshy areas.
4. The grasshopper mouse lives in plains or deserts.
5. They eat insects and scorpions.
6. The pygmy mouse is the smallest mouse in the world.
7. Field mice eat mainly plants and insects.
8. Some mice dig burrows or live in hollow logs.
9. The house mouse is the most common type.
10. White mice are used as pets.

Proper Nouns

A **proper noun** names a specific person, place, or thing. Proper nouns begin with a capital letter. A proper noun like Mexico City may have more than one word. Begin each word in a proper noun with a capital letter.

Example: Mr. Larson, Andrew, Chicago, Sears Tower

Directions: Read the nouns listed below. Write the proper nouns in the blanks provided.

family	dog	Jessica
July	street	teacher
man	Eiffel Tower	Drew School
Atlanta	Civil War	table

Proper Nouns

__________ __________ __________

__________ __________ __________

Directions: Underline and capitalize the proper nouns from each sentence below. (The capital letters have been left out.)

1. My dentist, dr. goodroe, takes care of my teeth.
2. My friends jeffrey, john, and ann also go to dr. goodroe.
3. I live on peachtree street in atlanta, georgia.
4. december is my favorite month of the year.
5. Our family visited the grand canyon last summer.
6. uncle jonathan took me to the san diego zoo today.

Plural Nouns

A noun can name one or more than one person, place, or thing. A noun that names only one of these is called a **singular noun**. A noun that names more than one is a **plural noun.**

Example:

Singular	Plural
brother	brothers
parade	parades

Add *-es* to form the plural of a noun that ends in *-s, -sh, -ch,* or *-x.*

Example:

Singular	Plural
bus	buses
dish	dishes
bunch	bunches
ax	axes

Directions: Change each singular noun to a plural noun.

Singular	Plural	Singular	Plural
1. hat		**13.** clock	
2. shoe		**14.** bird	
3. coat		**15.** store	
4. box		**16.** pass	
5. trunk		**17.** student	
6. sister		**18.** chair	
7. dress		**19.** floor	
8. friend		**20.** duck	
9. boy		**21.** church	
10. beach		**22.** fox	
11. brush		**23.** boat	
12. lunch		**24.** drum	

Singular Possessive Nouns

How do you show that a person owns something? One way to show ownership is to use a **singular possessive noun**. Add an **apostrophe** (') and an -*s* to singular nouns to show ownership.

Example:

the dog belonging to the boy — the **boy's** dog
the bowl belonging to the dog — the **dog's** bowl

Directions: Rewrite each group of words with possessive nouns to make them show ownership.

1. the teacher of the class ______________________
2. the tail of the dog ______________________
3. the leaves of the tree ______________________
4. the shoes of the athlete ______________________
5. the books of the student ______________________
6. the uncle of the boy ______________________
7. the papers of the teacher ______________________
8. the dresses of the woman ______________________
9. the bat of the ballplayer ______________________
10. the leader of the band ______________________

Plural Possessive Nouns

Plural possessive nouns show that a person, animal, or thing owns or has something. Add an **apostrophe** (') to make plural nouns possessive.

Example: classes — classes' books
players — players' caps

Directions: Change the underlined word to show possession by adding an apostrophe. Write the plural possessive form on the line.

1. The babies gifts were very cute. ______________
2. The students grades were good. ______________
3. The watches crystals were cracked. ______________
4. My grandparents attic is neat. ______________
5. His brothers bicycles were stolen. ______________
6. My aunts children came for a visit. ______________
7. The trees leaves are changing. ______________
8. The dogs tails were wagging. ______________
9. Those boys toys are in the driveway. ______________

Directions: Underline all nouns. Change singular nouns to plural nouns where necessary. Capitalize all proper nouns.

Mammoth Cave National Park

mammoth cave is part of the world's longest known cave system. It is surrounded by mammoth cave national park. The park is located in central kentucky. The green and nolin river flow through the park. This national park was started in 1941.

mammoth cave is sometimes called one of the wonder of the western hemisphere. The cave is located on a ridge made mainly of limestone. There are 12 mile of corridors through which visitors can be guided. The cave has five levels. The lowest level is 360 feet below the surface of the earth. There are many rock in the cave which have interesting colors and shapes.

Several lake, rivers, and waterfalls can be found in the cave. The largest river, echo river, varies in width from 20 to 60 feet and 5 to 25 feet in depth. Strange, eyeless fish live in echo river. They are about three inches long and are colorless. Beetles and crayfish are two other blind creature that live in mammoth cave.

What are pronouns?

A **pronoun** is a word that takes the place of one or more nouns.

Pronoun Tips	Singular	Plural
To talk about yourself, use these pronouns:	I, me	we, us
To talk to another person, use this pronoun:	you	you
To talk about another person or thing, use these:	he, him, she, her, it	they, them

Directions: Underline the pronoun(s) in these sentences.

1. Tomorrow we are going to the skating rink.
2. My sister and I love to ice skate.
3. You should try skating. It is enjoyable.
4. They will join us later at the rink.
5. He and she will join them later.

Directions: Write a pronoun to replace the underlined word or words.

6. Kelly and Monica laughed and sang. ____________
7. The dog chased the cat around the block. ____________
8. Where did your brother learn to skate? ____________
9. My sister and I finished our chores early. ____________

Identifying Pronouns

Directions: Circle the pronouns that can be used for each noun.

Nouns	Pronouns		
1. Anita	she	he	her
2. Nicholas	it	him	he
3. forks	them	it	they
4. doll	her	them	it
5. Boston	he	it	she
6. sister	you	she	her
7. friends	they	them	it
8. desk	it	he	her
9. Dr. Ross	she	he	her
10. trees	him	they	them

Directions: Choose the pronoun that could be used to replace the underlined word(s).

11. Albert wanted to go to the music store alone. (Him, He)

12. John, take these flowers to Mrs. Robertson. (You, They)

13. What song did your sister sing in the choir? (she, her)

14. Walter and I ran in the marathon race. (We, Us)

15. Put the dishes in the dishwasher. (it, they)

16. The teacher gave the class a test. (they, them)

17. Mrs. Stewart asked Jerome to stay after class. (him, he)

Subject Pronouns

A pronoun can be used as a **subject** of a sentence. The subject tells whom or what the sentence is about. Not all pronouns can be used as subjects. Only the **subject pronouns** listed below can be used as the subjects of sentences.

Subject Pronouns					
Singular	I	you	he	she	it
Plural	we	you	they		

Directions: Underline the subject pronoun in each sentence.

1. I saw a squirrel run across the yard and up the tree.

2. It lives in the oak tree next door in my neighbor's yard.

3. We enjoy watching the squirrels chase each other.

4. They eat seeds, nuts, berries, and insects.

5. You can come watch the squirrels tomorrow.

Directions: Replace the underlined words with a subject pronoun.

6. Gray squirrels live mainly in tree hollows.

7. My brother and I nicknamed one squirrel Bushy.

8. Bushy performs for us in the backyard each day.

9. Ann, my next door neighbor, also enjoys the squirrels.

Object Pronouns

Remember, subject pronouns can be used as the subject of a sentence. Use an **object pronoun** (*me*, *you*, *him*, *her*, *it*, *us*, and *them*) after an action verb, such as *run*, *jump*, *walk*, *swim*, and *show*, or words such as *to*, *of*, *for*, *with*, and *at*.

Example: The young girl ran toward **me**. (me = object pronoun after the action verb *ran*)

Jeff went to the zoo with **him**. (him = object pronoun after the word *with*)

Directions: In the following sentences, the subject pronoun is listed to the left of the sentence. Write the object pronoun in the blank provided.

they **1.** The chef showed _______ how to make the cake.

I **2.** Please give this new CD to _______.

he **3.** Marcus walked with _______ to school.

she **4.** Anna's dog ran quickly to _______.

they **5.** We wanted to give _______ one of the puppies.

I **6.** Arthur showed his new sneakers to _______.

we **7.** My father gave _______ our allowance.

he **8.** Sam's brother raced _______ to the finish line.

Possessive Pronouns

Possessive pronouns show ownership and take the place of a possessive noun. Use the pronouns *her, his, your, my, and its* to take the place of singular possessive nouns.

Example: John's book is due at the library.
His book is due at the library.

Use the pronouns *their, your,* and *our* to take the place of plural possessive nouns.

Example: Bob and Andre's sister called them for dinner.
Their sister called them for dinner.

Directions: Write the correct possessive pronoun in the blank.

1. _____ Aunt Sarah is coming for a visit. (My, She, They)

2. Is that _____ silver car in the driveway? (he, it, your)

3. Renee thought it was _____ suitcase. (she, hers, our)

4. Which one of these sweaters is ______? (his, I, you)

5. _____ team was winning the game. (Their, I, They)

6. Give me _____ ideas for the new club. (me, you, your)

7. You read your story; let me read ____ story. (I, we, my)

8. David wanted _____ video game returned. (he, his, him)

9. This stereo is not yours; it is _____. (I, she, mine)

10. _____ favorite movie is *Aladdin*. (She, Her, It)

Pronouns in Contractions

A **contraction** is the combined form of two words. Some contractions are formed by combining a pronoun and a verb. Use an **apostrophe** (') to replace the letter or letters that are omitted. Study the following chart containing contractions formed from pronouns.

Pronoun and Verb	Contraction
I have	I've
he has	he's
she has	she's
it has	it's
you have	you've
we have	we've
they have	they've
I had	I'd
you had	you'd
he had	he'd
we had	we'd
I am	I'm
he is	he's
she is	she's
it is	it's
you are	you're
we are	we're
they are	they're
I will	I'll
you will	you'll
she will	she'll
they will	they'll

Directions: What contractions are formed from the following pairs of words?

1. you had ______________

2. he has ______________

3. it has ______________

Pronouns in Contractions

Directions: Write the two words for each underlined contraction.

Example: She'll finish the exercise before me. **(She will)**

1. We're planning our summer vacation.
2. I'll show you the best route to Phoenix, Arizona.
3. Bev said she'll take care of the dog while we are gone.
4. My brother told me he's trying out for the team.
5. He'd better practice before the tryouts.
6. Someone told me it's difficult to make the team.
7. They'll let us know next Saturday who made the team.
8. I'm sure Jennifer and Frederick are on the team.
9. The teacher said she's giving back the test today.
10. You'll probably make an A on the test.
11. However, I'll be lucky if I make a B.
12. Sam and Terry are sure they're getting A's.
13. We'd better study hard for next week's test.
14. You'd better believe my parents will be happy.

Reviewing Pronouns

Directions: Write the best answer in the blank.

1. Let ____ take his turn using the computer.
A. it B. his C. him D. he

2. Where did you say _____ was located?
A. it B. his C. him D. he

3. Ask _____ sister to join our club.
A. it B. his C. him D. he

4. Did you know that ____ is playing baseball?
A. it B. his C. him D. he

5. _____ wanted us to join the baseball team.
A. They B. Them C. We D. Us

6. ____ told them our mother had to approve.
A. They B. Them C. We D. Us

7. Uncle Henry showed _____ how to catch a ball.
A. they B. he C. we D. us

8. The coach told _____ that they made the team.
A. they B. them C. we D. he

9. Don will bring ____ new video camera.
A. his B. her C. they D. you

10. Mary said ______ come to our first game.
A. he'll B. she'll C. they'll D. it'll

11. ____ getting to be very late in the day.
A. It's B. I'd C. We'll D. They'll

What are verbs?

A **verb** is a word that tells what people or things are doing or have done.

Margaret **borrowed** my new pencil.
The candle **burned** during the storm.

Directions: Circle the verbs in the following sentences.

1. Six horses pulled the covered wagons westward.
2. The settlers built the first covered wagons in Conestoga, Pennsylvania.
3. The wagons carried heavy loads across the prairies.
4. Their large wheels helped them over ruts and through mud on the prairie roads.
5. A large canvas cover protected against bad weather.
6. Some people called covered wagons "prairie schooners."
7. The wagon's white top looked like a sailing ship.
8. Most prairie schooners had a canvas cover over arched hoops.
9. Wagon trains carried pioneers to Utah, Oregon, and California in the late 1840s.
10. During the California Gold Rush of 1849, more than 12,000 wagons crossed the Missouri River.

Words that show action are called **action verbs**. An ***action verb*** tells what a person or thing is doing.

Example: The dog **stretched** his legs after his nap.
The children **ran, jumped,** and **played**.

Directions: Underline the action verb(s) in the following sentences.

1. Robots perform a wide variety of tasks.
2. Robots weld, drill, and paint automobile body parts.
3. In factories, they also produce plastic food containers and wrap ice cream bars.
4. Some robots even assemble electronic circuits and watches.
5. A typical robot performs a task by following instructions.
6. Workers control robots by using stored instructions.
7. Robots search the sea floor for new discoveries.
8. Some robots explore other planets.
9. Engineers equip some robots with television cameras and electronic sensors.

Recognizing Linking Verbs (Special Verb "Be")

The verbs *am*, *is*, *are*, *was*, and *were* are forms of the verb *be*. These verbs, called **linking verbs,** do not show action. Instead of showing action, they link the subject to the rest of the sentence.

Subject	Singular	Subject	Plural
I	am, was	We	are, were
You	are	You	were
She, He, It	is, was	They	are, were
Maria	is, was	Cats	are, were

Example: Susan **is** eight years old.
They **were** on a science field trip.

Directions: Underline the *be* verbs (linking verbs) in each sentence.

1. Nigeria is the most populated country in Africa.

2. There are more than 250 ethnic groups in Nigeria.

3. Lagos is the largest city in Nigeria.

4. Lagos was the capital city, but now it is Abuja.

5. Dairy cattle are scarce along the coast because of the tsetse fly.

6. Did you know that the Nok people were among the first to live in Nigeria?

7. The main foods in Nigeria are yams, corn, beans, and rice.

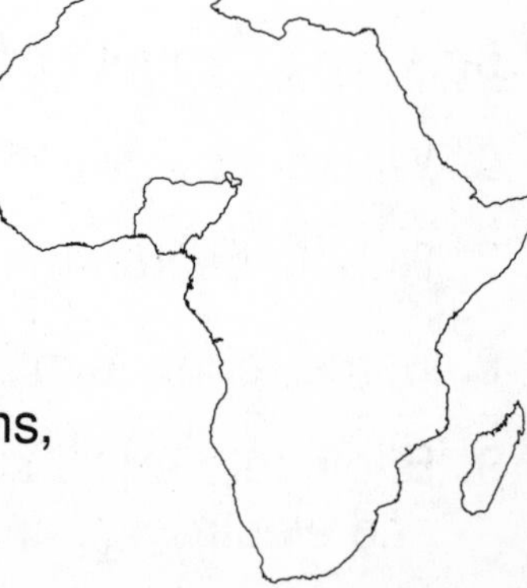

Verbs in the Present Tense

Besides showing action or linking subjects to the rest of the sentence, verbs indicate time. This time is called **tense**. There are three tenses of time: **present**, **past**, and **future**.

Present tense verbs show action that is **happening now**. Verbs in the present tense have two forms. The form you use depends on what the subject of the sentence is.

→ Add -*s* to the verb when the subject is singular.

Example: A spider **spins** silk to build a web.

→ Do **not** add -*s* to the verb when the subject is plural.

Example: Spiders **spin** silk to build webs.

Directions: Underline the correct present tense verb.

1. Spiders (use, uses) their webs to catch insects for food.
2. Some spiders do not (make, makes) webs.
3. The bolas spider (spin, spins) a single line of silk with a drop of sticky silk at the end.
4. This spider (swing, swings) the line at an insect.
5. It (trap, traps) the insect on the sticky ball.
6. All spiders (has, have) fangs.
7. Spiders (use, uses) their fangs and poison to capture animals for food.

Verbs in the Past Tense

Verbs in the present tense tell about actions that are happening now. A verb that tells about an action that **has already happened** is in the **past tense**.

- Add -***ed*** to most verbs: talk**ed**, jump**ed**, walk**ed**
- Change *y* to *i* and add -***ed*** to verbs that end with a consonant and y: study = stud**ied**, worry = worr**ied**
- Drop the e and add -***ed*** to verbs that end with *e*: use = us**ed**, prove = prov**ed**, stare = star**ed**
- Double the consonant and add -***ed*** to most verbs that end with one vowel and one consonant: pop = pop**ped**

Directions: Change the verb in parentheses to past tense.

_______ **1.** Marco Polo (travel) in Asia in the late 1200s.

_______ **2.** Marco, his father, and his uncle (arrive) in the summer capital of Kublai Khan in 1275.

_______ **3.** Marco (roam) through China for 17 years.

_______ **4.** Khan (allow) them to sail home in 1292.

_______ **5.** Marco (stop) in Persia on a diplomatic mission.

_______ **6.** People (study) Polo's written account of his travels through Asia.

_______ **7.** *The Travels of Marco Polo* was (receive) with astonishment.

Verbs in the Future Tense

Verbs tell about actions in the present and the past. Verbs can also show an action that will happen in the future. This form of the verb is called **future tense**. Use the special verb *will* to write about the future.

Present	The dogs **play** in the backyard.
Past	The dogs **played** in the backyard.
Future	The dogs **will play** in the backyard.

Directions: Write the correct future tense of each verb.

1. Oscar ____________ a report about Marco Polo. (write)

2. Jose ______________ for his math test. (study)

3. Bryan and Marcos ______________ in the concert. (sing)

4. The dog _____________ the soup bone for dinner. (enjoy)

5. The class _____________ the next field trip. (plan)

Directions: Write whether each underlined verb is in the present, past, or future tense.

________ **6.** I <u>shopped</u> at the grocery for my mother.

________ **7.** Mother <u>wanted</u> eggs, chocolate, and milk.

________ **8.** My mother <u>bakes</u> delicious brownies.

________ **9.** I <u>will eat</u> some of the brownies she makes.

________ **10.** I <u>will share</u> the brownies with my brother.

Helping Verbs

Use the verbs *has, have,* and *had* to help other verbs show an action in the past. These verbs are called **helping verbs**. For most verbs that have a helping verb, add the letters *-**ed***.

→ Use *has* with a singular subject and with *he, she,* or *it.*

Example: She **has painted** a picture of the sunset.

→ Use *had* with a singular or plural subject.

Example: They **had painted** many sunsets.

→ Use *have* with a plural subject and *I, you, we,* or *they.*

Example: The artists **have painted** many sunsets.

Directions: In the following, underline the helping verb(s).

1. Marilyn has enjoyed the art class.

2. Nathan and I have learned much about painting.

3. Charles had wished he had taken the art class.

Directions: Underline the correct helping verb.

4. The teacher (has, have) taught art for twelve years.

5. Many of her friends (has, have) taken the art class.

6. Her friends (has, had) painted before this class.

7. The paintings (has, have) been chosen for the contest.

Irregular Verbs

Some verbs form the past tense in a special way. These verbs also have a special spelling when used with a helping verb. Verbs that do not add -***ed*** to form the past tense are **irregular verbs**.

Present	Past	Past with *has, have,* or *had*
do	did	has, have, or had done
run	ran	has, have, or had run
go	went	has, have, or had gone
come	came	has, have, or had come
see	saw	has, have, or had seen

Directions: Underline the correct verb form in each sentence.

1. The tennis player (run, ran) up and down the court.

2. We (seen, saw) three professional tennis players.

3. They had (come, came) to play in the tournament.

4. Serena Williams (go, went) to receive her trophy.

5. I have (saw, seen) many tennis matches this year.

6. One male tennis player (ran, run) into the net and fell.

7. I would love to (go, went) to Wimbledon to see the Lawn Tennis Championship.

8. Will you (come, came) to see me play tennis?

Irregular Verbs

The **irregular verbs** *begin*, *eat*, *give*, *grow*, *sing*, and *take* also have a special spelling to show past tense. Their spelling changes when used with *has*, *have*, or *had*.

Present	Past	Past with *has*, *have*, or *had*
begin	began	has, have, or had begun
eat	ate	has, have, or had eaten
give	gave	has, have, or had given
grow	grew	has, have, or had grown
sing	sang	has, have, or had sung
take	took	has, have, or had taken

Directions: Underline the correct verb for each sentence.

1. Koalas (eaten, eat) eucalyptus leaves for their meals.

2. The robin (sing, sang) outside my window this morning.

3. Thomas had (gave, given) his dog a bath.

4. The squirrels (taken, took) the bird food from the feeder.

5. Please (begin, began) your piano lessons now.

6. The baby had (grew, grown) two inches since I saw him.

7. I have (took, taken) piano lesson for three years.

8. The tomato plants (grown, grew) quickly after the rain.

9. Quiet please, the concert has (began, begun).

Contractions with *Not*

A contraction is the shortened form of two words. An **apostrophe (')** takes the place of any letter or letters that are left out. Many contractions are formed with the word *not*. Words with *not* are called **negative words**.

Contractions Using *Not*

do not	don't	could not	couldn't
were not	weren't	should not	shouldn't
cannot	can't	would not	wouldn't
is not	isn't	was not	wasn't
had not	hadn't	did not	didn't
are not	aren't	has not	hasn't
does not	doesn't	have not	haven't

Directions: Write the contraction for the word or words.

1. cannot __________
2. have not __________
3. could not __________
4. were not __________
5. does not __________
6. should not __________

Directions: Write the words for the underlined contractions.

7. Mother said I <u>couldn't</u> go to the park today.

8. Richard <u>doesn't</u> like to play basketball.

9. Jessica and Melvin <u>haven't</u> had supper.

10. Marilyn <u>can't</u> sing very well.

Reviewing Verbs

Directions: Study the list below. Underline only the **verbs**.

run	are	brownies	wouldn't
koala	used	sang	began
pulled	cattle	Bryan	factory
Robert	trapped	enjoying	baseball
settlers	spider	Alaska	wagon
carried	lunch	learned	helped
robot	stops	saw	is
searched	China	came	wasn't
planet	spins	tomato	web
Nigeria	Marco	Richard	spider

Directions: Underline the correct verb in each sentence.

1. The baseball players (play, played) in the park last night.

2. The boy who was injured was (carry, carried) off the field.

3. We have (saw, seen) other players injured during games.

4. That train (stop, stops) at this station at 1:00 every day.

5. I had (watch, watched) the train pull into the station.

6. Charles (begin, began) to collect trains when he was five.

7. I (have, has) enjoyed looking at his collection of trains.

8. There (wasn't, weren't) any warning before the accident.

Reviewing Verbs

Directions: Read the sentence. Choose the letter of the underlined word or words that are verbs.

___ **1.** The boys and girls clapped after the performance.
A B C D

___ **2.** Some of the actors appeared in front of the stage.
A B C D

___ **3.** Other actors were seen in the lobby.
A B C D

___ **4.** After the play, we stopped for ice cream.
A B C D

Directions: Write the letter of the sentence that is written correctly.

___ **5.** A. Jerry gone to see his uncle.
B. His uncle weren't at home.
C. Then Jerry walked to the corner store.
D. After going to the store, he were walking home.

___ **6.** A. Shane's computer had a virus.
B. His brother has took it to the repair store.
C. The technician telled him he could fix it.
D. Shane were wondering how much it would cost.

___ **7.** A. We riding our bicycles to the library.
B. Our teacher assign us a report for Monday.
C. The librarian helping us with the research.
D. We were able to finish our report on time.

___ **8.** A. Marcia go to the library to find a book.
B. My mother singed in the church choir.
C. Mark's train jumped the track in the playroom.
D. Didn't you walked to school today?

Noun, Pronoun, Verb Crossword

Directions: Complete the puzzle using the clues. Choose from the following words: *contraction*, *possessive pronoun*, *past tense*, *common noun*, *subject pronoun*, *future tense*, *object pronoun*, *action verb*, and *proper noun*.

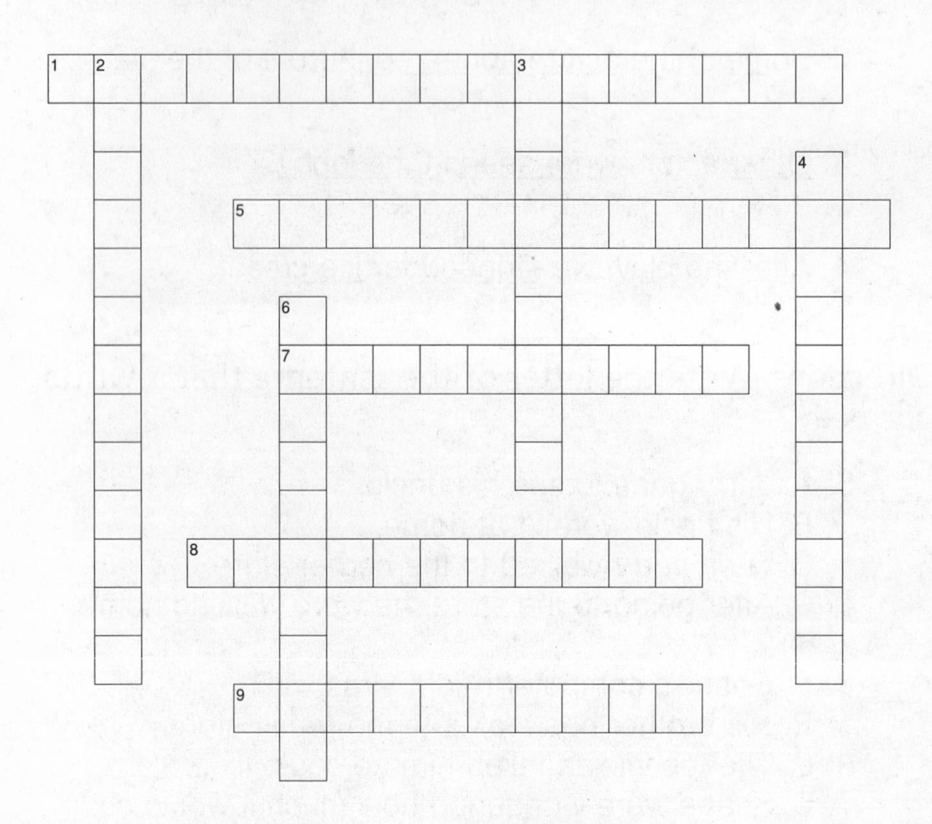

Across

1. our

5. they

7. raccoon

8. can't

9. New York City

Down

2. me

3. made

4. will study

6. walk

What are adjectives?

An **adjective** is a word that describes or tells about nouns. Adjectives tell **what kind** (*big, blue, high*), **how many** (*one, all, few*), or **which one** (*each, any, that, the*).

Example: Brazil is **the fifth largest** country in **the** world. **The largest** river in Brazil is **the** Amazon.

Directions: Underline the adjectives.

1. The Amazon rain forest is the world's largest rain forest.

2. Most of Brazil's big cities are located near the coast.

3. Rural people usually work on large farms.

4. Most families live in one- or two-room stone or adobe houses with clay tile roofs.

5. In poor areas of cities, the main foods are beans, rice, and *manioc*.

6. People in the cities enjoy eating juicy hamburgers, wheat bread, and a variety of meats.

7. Soccer is the most popular sport in Brazil.

8. People enjoy relaxing at the many beautiful beaches.

9. Many colorful festivals take place in Brazil.

Adjectives — "What Kind" or "Which One"

Using **adjectives** can make your sentences more interesting. They add details to make your meaning clearer. Adjectives tell **what kind** (*big, blue, high*) or **which one** (*each, any, this, that*).

Example: The angry man gave the waitress a small tip.

(**What kind** of man?) (**What kind** of tip?)

This river, the Nile River, is located in Egypt.

(**Which one**?)

Draw an arrow to the adjectives that describes each underlined noun.

1. Most gas balloons carry a heavy drag rope.
2. This rope is used just before landing.
3. Some person on the ground grabs the rope to help land the balloon.
4. Two papermakers from France began experiments with hot-air balloons in the 1700s.
5. The Montgolfiers started experimenting by filling paper bags with smoke.
6. Each experiment helped the brothers learn more about hot-air balloons.
7. In 1999, a British pilot became one of the first balloonists to fly around the world without landing.

Adjectives — "How Many"

You have learned that adjectives can tell **what kind** or **which one**. Adjectives such as *one*, *five*, *several*, *many*, or *few* tell **how many**. An adjective that tells **how many** comes **before the noun** it is describing.

Example: The teacher gave the boy **two** pencils.
Several students did not have pencils.

Directions: Underline the adjectives that tell how many.

1. Many doctors are located in this building.

2. After the game, three students walked home.

3. Our vacation lasted seven days.

4. On our vacation, we passed through several towns.

5. In our class, there were thirty students.

Directions: Write an adjective in each blank. Do not use the same adjective more than once.

6. There were _____ basketballs left on the court.

7. _______ players received trophies at the banquet.

8. At the game, _______ cheerleaders made things exciting.

9. The other team had _______ players injured.

10. My _____ favorite teams are playing tonight.

The words *a*, *an*, and *the* are special adjectives called **articles**.

With singular nouns...

Use ***a*** before words that begin with a consonant sound.

Use ***an*** before words that begin with a vowel sound or a silent *h*.

Use ***the*** if the noun names a particular person, place, or thing.

With plural nouns...

Use **the** before a plural noun.

A hippopotamus cooled himself in **the** river.
An elephant gave himself **a** mud bath.
The zebras protected their young from **the** lions.

Directions: Complete the paragraph below using the articles *a*, *an*, and *the*.

Stalactite

___ beautiful stone formation found in some limestone caves is ___ stalactite. Stalactites hang from ____ walls or roofs of ____ caves. Some resemble draperies or straws with __ hole through the center, but most look like ___ icicle.

Most stalactites are formed by water dripping in ____ cave. When ____ water drips, it leaves behind __ small amount of minerals. These minerals build up very slowly and form stalactites. Examples of ____ stalactite can be found in ____ Carlsbad Caverns in New Mexico.

Using Adjectives

Write three adjectives that describe each pictured noun below. Do not use the same adjective more than once.

flowers ______ ______ ______	**hamburger** ______ ______ ______
dog ______ ______ ______	**hands** ______ ______ ______
building ______ ______ ______	**train** ______ ______ ______

Comparing with Adjectives

Adjectives are words that describe nouns. Adjectives can also be used to show how people, places, or things are alike or different.

For most adjectives, add -***er*** to the end of the word when you want to compare two people, places, or things.

Example: That dog is **bigger** than this one.

When comparing three or more persons, places, or things, add -***est*** to most words.

Example: This is the **biggest** dog of all.

Directions: Underline the correct word.

1. My sandwich is (bigger, biggest) than Matthew's sandwich.

2. Angela's hair was the (longer, longest) of all the girls in our class.

3. That cat has the (longer, longest) tail of any cat that I have ever seen.

4. Australia is a (smaller, smallest) continent than Asia.

5. The Pacific Ocean is the (larger, largest) ocean on Earth.

6. My grandson, Chandler, is one of the (cuter, cutest) babies I have ever seen.

7. My classroom is (colder, coldest) than your classroom.

What are adverbs?

An **adverb** is a word that can describe or tell more about a verb. Adverbs can tell **how, when,** or **where** an action happened. Many adverbs end in *-ly*. Adverbs can come before or after the verbs they describe.

Example: The boys and girls sat <u>quietly</u>. (**after** the verb)
How did they sit? (quietly)
Kim <u>quickly</u> opened the door. (**before** the verb)
How did she open the door? (quickly)

Directions: Underline the adverbs in the following sentences.

1. Three kittens happily played with the ball of yarn.
2. Mrs. Lee carefully pulled the weeds in the garden.
3. Tanisha and Melody were walking quickly to the store.
4. Did you see the horse as he jumped the fence gracefully?
5. Suddenly, the dog began to bark at the raccoon in the tree.
6. Angelica, please set the table neatly!
7. The children ate their snacks hungrily.
8. Slowly, the people entered the museum to see the new dinosaur exhibit.
9. We watched as the mother gently picked up the baby.
10. The cows entered the barn mooing noisily.

Adverbs That Tell "When"

Adverbs can tell how an action occurs. They can also tell **when** an action happens.

Adverbs that tell **when** an action happens	
always	first
early	next
now	later
today	then
soon	yesterday
tomorrow	often

Directions: Underline the adverbs in the following sentences.

1. Michael is always on time for school.

2. Yesterday, I walked to the grocery store with my sister.

3. The teacher often surprises us with treats.

4. Angelica is coming to my house today after school.

5. Now we are going to begin our history project.

Directions: Underline the adverbs and write whether the adverb tells *how* or *when* in the blank.

________ **6.** My mom took me to the dentist today.

________ **7.** I anxiously agreed to open my mouth for him.

________ **8.** Dr. Kelly carefully checked my teeth.

________ **9.** I knew that this checkup would be over soon.

Adverbs That Tell "Where"

Adverbs can tell how and when an action occurs. They can also tell **where** an action happens.

Adverbs that tell **where** an action happens	
ahead	nearby
around	out
away	outside
everywhere	there
far	up
here	upstairs

Example: The stadium is located nearby.
Where is the stadium located? (nearby)

Directions: Underline the adverbs in the following sentences.

1. The coach said we should run outside to warm up.

2. Some of the team members thought it was too far.

3. There are the soccer balls we will use for today's practice.

4. Nancy told us to kick the ball ahead of us and into the goal.

Directions: Write an adverb that tells **where** in the blank. Do not use the same word more than once.

5. Go and get the suitcase ______________.

6. When visitors came to see the puppies, the mother dog stayed ___________ and kept watch.

7. We are supposed to play _________ this morning.

Using your imagination, complete the following story with adverbs. Remember: adverbs tell *when*, *where*, or *how*.

Rhinoceros

The rhinoceros had two horns. She __________ used them for digging and fighting. The mother rhinoceros walked ________ in the grass looking for food. The rhinoceros eats _________ bulbs, grass, and other plants. She was _________ protective of her baby. The baby wandered ____________ trying to investigate his surroundings. __________ the mother nudged the baby back into the tall grass for protection.

_____________ the mother had to fight enemies to protect her baby. She used her horns, which are made ___________ of the same protein found in hair. The rhinoceros ___________ depends on its sense of smell because it has poor eyesight.

___________ the baby depends on his mother for food. ___________ as the baby grows he learns to find food on his own. This baby is about two or two-and-a-half years old. ___________ he will leave his mother to live on his own.

Adverbs tell *where*, *when*, or *how* something happens. Adding adverbs to a sentence can make it more interesting.

Example: The girl sang **beautifully** in the talent show.
The audience clapped.
The audience clapped **loudly**.

Adverbs can be placed in different places in a sentence.

Example: **Suddenly,** the play ended.
The play ended **suddenly**.
The play **suddenly** ended.

Directions: Copy the following paragraph on another piece of paper. Choose adverbs from the box below or choose some of your own to make the sentences more interesting.

rapidly	then	finally
extremely	quickly	later
suddenly	eagerly	carefully
slowly	next	soon

The Train Trip

I had to pack for our trip to my grandmother's house. Mother said that we were leaving today. Mother and I boarded the train. I was excited about our trip. We walked down the aisle to our seats. The train began to move. It moved down the tracks. We were on our way. I would see my grandmother. The train ride ended. We exited the train.

Adverb and Adjective Review

Directions: Read each sentence. Write the letter that identifies the **adjective** in the sentence.

___ **1.** The bluebird flew to the birdbath.

A. bluebird

B. flew

C. the

___ **2.** Pretty cardinals also enjoyed the bath.

A. Pretty

B. cardinals

C. enjoyed

___ **3.** Soon, the robin flew to the cool water.

A. Soon

B. robin

C. cool

___ **4.** Three baby birds stayed in the nest.

A. Three

B. stayed

C. nest

Directions: Read each sentence. Write the letter that identifies the **adverb** in the sentence.

___ **5.** The blue jay noisily chased the birds.

A. blue jay

B. noisily

C. chased

___ **6.** Two mockingbirds sang beautifully in the trees.

A. Two

B. mockingbirds

C. beautifully

___ **7.** The robins ate the worms hungrily.

A. ate

B. worms

C. hungrily

___ **8.** Finally, all of the birds flew away.

A. Finally

B. all

C. flew

Adjective or Adverb?

Remember: **Adjectives** tell "which one," "how many," or "what kind" as they describe nouns.

Example: **Those** dogs ran. (Which dogs?)
Those **three** dogs ran. (How many dogs?)
Those three **fluffy** dogs ran. (What kind of dogs?)

Adverbs tell "how," "when," or "where" something happens.

Example: The dogs ran **quickly**. (How did they run?)
Now the dogs ran quickly. (When did they run?)
Now the dogs ran **away** quickly. (Where did they run?)

Directions: Read each sentence. Identify the underlined word as either an adjective (**ADJ**) or an adverb (**ADV**).

1. Three huge fish swam quickly through the water.
2. Many fishermen dream of catching huge fish.
3. Those new fishing rods worked extremely well.
4. Marsha and her brother got in that boat.
5. The small boat had to be paddled carefully.
6. Soon Marsha and her brother had each caught a fish.
7. Their fish wriggled rapidly on their lines.
8. I caught a small, smelly fish.

9. Each person caught at least one fish.

Identifying Parts of Speech

In each sentence, identify the part of speech (noun, verb, adjective, or adverb) for the underlined word and write it in the blank provided.

Example: A butterfly is a type of insect. **noun**

1. The mouth of a butterfly is a long tube called a proboscis. ___________

2. Butterflies go through four stages in their development. ___________

3. The first stage a butterfly goes through is the egg. ___________

4. Next is the larva stage, when it is called a caterpillar. ___________

5. When it is time, the caterpillar spins a cocoon, the third stage. ___________

6. The fourth stage is when the butterfly comes out of the cocoon. ___________

7. Adult butterflies eat many things: nectar, pollen, and fruit are just a few. ___________

8. Butterflies eat by uncoiling their long, tube-like mouths and sucking their food. ___________

9. The colors and patterns of the butterflies' wings help to protect them from enemies. ___________

10. Some butterflies have eyespots on their wings to fool their enemies. ___________

Mixed-up Parts of Speech

Directions: According to the following system, number each word in the groups of words; then copy the words in order.

1 = adjective; **2** = noun; **3** = verb; **4** = adverb

2 3 1 4
apple fell an down
An apple fell down.

1. dogs quickly ran three

____

2. fast a flew mockingbird

____

3. the mooed cow loudly

____

4. children quickly seven raced

____

5. thirteen happily puppies played

____

6. beautifully musician played the

____

7. landed butterfly a gently

____

8. twenty-five talked noisily students

____

Parts of Speech Review

Directions: Write the letter of the correct answer in the blank.

A. Identify the adverb.

A B C D
__ **1.** The red fox ran quickly.

A B C
__ **2.** Soon my aunt will
D
arrive.

A B C
__ **3.** Three red birds flew
D
fast.

A B C D
__ **4.** I will happily race my new bike.

B. Identify the noun.

A B C
__ **5.** My favorite aunt is
D
coming here.

A B C
__ **6.** Manuel plays for my
D
team.

A B C D
__ **7.** Al was very good.

A B
__ **8.** We were not able to
C D
play checkers.

C. Identify the verb.

A B C
__ **9.** Now the ball bounced
D
easily.

A B C
__ **10.** Nancy ran to the
D
store.

A B C
__ **11.** The large, green frog
D
hopped.

A B C D
__ **12.** Sing this song for me.

D. Identify the adjective.

A B C D
__ **13.** The cats purred quietly.

A B C D
__ **14.** My new dress was torn.

A B C D
__ **15.** Ann was a pretty girl.

A B C D
__ **16.** A dog ran home.

What is a sentence?

A **sentence** is a group of words that expresses a complete thought. A sentence must tell *who* or *what* in order to tell a complete thought. A sentence must also tell *what is* or *what happens*. Use a capital letter to begin a sentence.

Sentence = Rupert walked the dog.
Not a Sentence = Walked the dog.

Who or what?	**What is or what happens?**
Mrs. Peterson	baked a chocolate cake.
Her older brother	was playing basketball.

Directions: Identify which groups of words are sentences by writing the letter **S** in the blank. If the group of words does not form a sentence, write **NS**.

___ **1.** Alex Haley was an American author.

___ **2.** That became famous for his book *Roots*.

___ **3.** Beginning in the mid-1700s in Africa.

___ **4.** He described the history of his family.

___ **5.** Haley's ancestor Kunta Kinte.

___ **6.** Was kidnapped in Gambia in 1776.

___ **7.** Haley spent twelve years researching the book.

___ **8.** His fame grew after *Roots* appeared on television.

___ **9.** Grew up in Henning, Tennessee.

Statements and Questions

A sentence that tells something is a **statement**. A statement ends with a period(.).

Example: Joseph ran around the bases.

A sentence that asks something is a **question**. A question ends with a question mark(?).

Example: Did Joseph run around the bases?

Directions: Identify the following sentences as either statement (**S**) or question (**Q**).

___ **1.** Joseph was on the Orioles baseball team.

___ **2.** On which team are you playing?

___ **3.** Did you see Robert hit the home run?

___ **4.** Our team had a pizza party after the game.

Directions: Add the correct end punctuation to the following.

5. My dog Coco loves to sleep and eat

6. What do you think Coco's favorite foods are

7. Would you believe she eats vegetables and fruits

8. Coco loves to chase squirrels and cats from the yard

Writing Complete Sentences

To make their meaning clear, good writers use complete sentences. In some cases, a group of words that does not express a complete thought can be easily fixed. This can be done by putting incomplete sentences together to form a complete one.

The fifth planet from the sun.
Is the planet Jupiter.
The fifth planet from the sun is the planet Jupiter.

Sometimes incomplete sentences can be fixed by telling *who* or *what*.

Is made mainly of hydrogen and helium.
Jupiter is made mainly of hydrogen and helium.

Directions: Rewrite the following incomplete sentences and make them complete sentences.

1. Jupiter is covered by clouds. Which are organized into bands.

____

2. Has an unusual feature called the Great Red Spot.

____

3. A dark ring of dust. Was discovered by the *Voyager* spacecraft.

____

4. The planet Jupiter. Has at least sixteen moons.

____

Commands and Exclamations

A sentence that tells someone to do something is a **command**. A command ends with a period(.). A sentence that shows strong feeling, such as surprise, fear, or excitement, is an **exclamation**. An exclamation ends with an exclamation point(!).

Command = Wait until the bus stops.
Exclamation = Look at that huge rock!

Directions: For the following sentences, write **C** for command, or **E** for exclamation. Add the appropriate punctuation.

_____ **1.** Please open that screen door

_____ **2.** Don't let those flies in the house

_____ **3.** There's a swarm of bees in the house

_____ **4.** Get the bee spray quickly

_____ **5.** I'm allergic to bees

_____ **6.** Go in the other room and close the door

_____ **7.** Wait in the room until I call you

_____ **8.** Watch out

_____ **9.** Come out now

____ **10.** Make sure there are no more bees

Writing Sentences

Good writers use a variety of sentences including questions, commands, and exclamations. In the following sentences, notice how a statement can be changed into a question, a command, or an exclamation.

Example: Fred is helping me. (statement)
Is Fred helping me? (question)
Help me, Fred. (command)
Help me! (exclamation)

Directions: Change the sentences to one of the following: statement, question, command, or exclamation.

1. That dog is barking.

____

2. Mother baked some cookies.

____

3. Where is my brown jacket?

____

4. It is so hot today!

____

5. Pick up your toys.

____

6. John and Martha have been playing all day.

____

7. Is the computer in the office working?

____

Subjects in Sentences

You already know that a sentence is a group of words that tells a complete thought. The **subject** of the sentence tells what or whom the sentence is about. The subject can be one word or more than one word and usually comes at the beginning of the sentence.

David walked to the corner store.
He bought bacon and eggs.
The grocery store was crowded.
Most of the customers were bargain shoppers.

Directions: Underline the subject of each sentence.

1. Easter Island lies about 2,300 miles west of Chile.
2. It is famous as the site of enormous statues of people.
3. The early islanders created the most famous statues.
4. Most of the people are Polynesians.
5. More than 600 statues are scattered throughout the island.
6. The islanders used stone hand picks to carve the statues.
7. They set up the statues on raised platforms.
8. Huge, red stone cylinders sat on the heads of some of the statues like hats.

Predicates in Sentences

All sentences have two parts. The subject is one part of a sentence. The other part of the sentence is the **predicate**. The predicate of the sentence tells what the subject does or is. The predicate can be one word or more than one word.

Subject	Predicate
The Grand Canyon	extends 277 miles in Arizona.
The average rainfall	varies from 7 to 26 inches.
About 300 species of birds	are found in the Grand Canyon.

Directions: Underline the predicate in each sentence.

1. The Grand Canyon cuts through northwestern Arizona.
2. The canyon varies in width from less than 1 mile to 18 miles.
3. The Colorado River flows through the canyon.
4. The river formed the canyon over millions of years.
5. Some rocks in the deepest part date back two billion years.
6. The area has about 120 kinds of animals.
7. Ponderosa pine trees thrive on the canyon's rim.
8. Various Indian tribes have lived in the Grand Canyon.

Reviewing Sentences

Directions: Write **S** if the sentence is a complete thought. Write **NS** if the group of words does not form a sentence.

___ **1.** The Empire State Building built in 1930–1931.

___ **2.** It was situated on Fifth Avenue in New York City.

___ **3.** The tallest building in the world until 1971.

___ **4.** The building was opened during the Depression.

Directions: Write whether the sentence is a statement **(S)**, question **(Q)**, exclamation **(E)**, or command **(C)**. Put in the correct end mark.

___ **5.** Who paid to visit the observation deck

___ **6.** Please pay the fee to visit the top of the building

___ **7.** Much of its rentable space remained vacant for years

___ **8.** Don't get too close to the edge of the building

Directions: Underline the subject with one line and the predicate with two lines.

9. The Empire State Building cost $41 million.

10. The limestone and steel building was not original.

11. The original owners depended on sightseers to pay the building's taxes.

Capitalizing First Words

Perhaps one of the most important capitalization rules is one of the easiest to remember: **Always capitalize the first word of every sentence.** Remember: It does not matter whether the word is *I, you, he, me, a, an, the, Mrs. Powell, Memorial Day, Europe*, or *Amazon River*, the first word of every sentence is **always** capitalized.

Example: **S**he surprised me with a new computer.
My new computer has a flat screen.

Directions: Read the story about Jack London. As you read, write the capital letter above where it is needed.

considered by many to be America's finest author, Jack London was born on Market Street in San Francisco. his name at birth was John Griffith Chaney. he was the son of William Chaney, an astrologer and journalist. his father deserted Jack's mother, Flora, before Jack was born. later, Flora married John London, a Civil War veteran. much of Jack's youth was spent in Oakland, California, on the waterfront.

jack had little formal schooling. he attended school only through the eighth grade, although he was an avid reader. in later years, Jack returned to high school in Oakland and graduated.

he became the best selling, highest paid, and most popular American author of his time. his most notable book, *The Call of the Wild*, is considered an all-time classic.

Common & Proper Nouns

Nouns that name any person, place, or thing are called **common nouns**. A noun that names a particular person, place, or thing is called a **proper noun**. Proper nouns begin with a capital letter. Sometimes a proper noun, such as San Diego, may have more than one word. Remember: Begin each important word in a proper noun with a capital letter.

Common Noun	Proper Noun
The **boy** walked the dog.	**Sammy** walked the dog.
His **dog** went with him.	**Rover** went with him.
The **city** has a zoo.	**San Diego** has a zoo.

Directions: Read the nouns below. Circle the proper nouns.

president
Monday
park
Oak Street

Katherine
President Bush
Mr. Thomas
state

Piedmont Park
South Dakota
street
Robert

Directions: Underline the proper nouns in the following.

1. Saturn is the sixth planet in the solar system.

2. Like Jupiter, Saturn is a hydrogen/helium planet.

3. Saturn has 18 known moons; the largest is Titan.

4. Rings of clouds around Saturn were observed by *Voyager*.

Days, Months, and Holidays

The names of the **days** of the week and **months** of the year are capitalized.

Example: Monday Thursday Saturday
February July December

Sandra goes to dancing lessons every **T**uesday.
Joseph loves to go swimming during **J**uly.

The names of **holidays** are capitalized.

Example: **L**abor **D**ay **M**emorial **D**ay **P**resident's **D**ay

My family looks forward to **M**emorial **D**ay.

Directions: Rewrite these days of the week, months of the year, and holidays. Use capital letters where needed.

1. may — memorial day and mother's day

____

2. october — columbus day and halloween

____

3. february — valentine's day

____

4. december — christmas and hanukkah

____

5. january — new year's day and martin luther king day

____

6. monday, wednesday, thursday, saturday, sunday

____

____

Abbreviations and Titles

An **abbreviation** is a shortened form of a word. Most abbreviations begin with a capital letter and end with a period. You can abbreviate days of the week.

Example: **S**un. **M**on. **T**ues. **W**ed. **T**hurs. **F**ri. **S**at.

You can abbreviate the months of the year.

Example: **J**an. **F**eb. **M**ar. **A**pr. **A**ug. **S**ept. **O**ct. **N**ov. **D**ec.

Capitalize a **title** when it comes before the person's name. If the title is more than one word, capitalize every important word. Some titles may be written out or abbreviated. To show respect, some titles are capitalized when they are used in place of the person's name.

Example: titles — **P**resident Bush, **R**everend Thomas
Mr. = Mister **D**r. = Doctor **C**apt. = Captain

The first word, last word, and other important words in **titles** are capitalized.

Example: Book = *Where the Wild Things Are*
Movie = *Seabiscuit*
Poem = "**M**ary **H**ad a **L**ittle **L**amb"
Song = "**T**he **S**tar **S**pangled **B**anner"

Directions: Write each abbreviation and title correctly.

1. tues

2. oct

3. mr david park

4. *the wizard of oz*

5. *treasure island*

6. "over the rainbow"

7. rev mark bowling

8. miss wendy clark

Place Names

Capitalize the major words in **geographical names.**

Example: **M**iami **C**olorado **G**ermany
Europe **L**ake **S**uperior **M**ount **R**ushmore

Our family drove to **S**outh **D**akota in August to visit **M**ount **R**ushmore.

Capitalize the names of **streets, roads, places, buildings,** and **monuments.**

Example: **O**akland **A**venue **T**imes **S**quare
Lincoln **M**emorial **S**ears **T**owers

Piedmont **H**ospital is on **P**eachtree **S**treet.

Directions: Insert capital letters in the following sentences where needed.

1. my friend Jonathan hiked through the grand canyon.

2. sarah is a nurse at northside hospital on johnson road.

3. when we were in chicago, we swam in lake michigan.

4. in paris, there is a famous church called notre dame.

5. last year, our class visited the louvre, a famous art museum.

End Marks

A **statement** is a sentence that tells something. A statement ends with a **period**.

Example: Donald climbed the mountain in Yellowstone Park.

A **command** is a sentence that tells or asks someone to do something. A command ends with a **period.**

Example: Please pack your bags for mountain climbing.

A **question** is a sentence that asks something. A question ends with a **question mark.**

Example: Did Donald follow the trail?

An **exclamation** is a sentence that shows strong feeling. An exclamation ends with an **exclamation mark.**

Example: Watch out for that brown bear!

Directions: Use the correct end mark for the following.

1. Be sure to take water and food with you

2. Wear warm clothes while mountain climbing

3. How many students are mountain climbing today

4. Are you afraid to go mountain climbing

5. You will see beautiful scenery while mountain climbing

6. Wow, what a breathtaking view that is

7. Is it time to eat lunch

8. Look at the wild flowers growing in the distance

Abbreviations

Some words have a shortened form called an **abbreviation**. Most abbreviations begin with a capital letter and end with a period. Here are some common abbreviations:

Titles	**Mr.**	Mister	**Mrs.**	married woman
	Jr.	Junior	**Ms.**	any woman
	Sr.	Senior	**Dr.**	Doctor
Addresses	**Rd.**	Road	**Co.**	Company
	St.	Street	**P.O.**	Post Office
	Ave.	Avenue	**Blvd.**	Boulevard
Months	**Jan.**	January	**Sept.**	September
	Apr.	April	**Nov.**	November
Days	**Sun.**	Sunday	**Wed.**	Wednesday
	Tues.	Tuesday	**Thurs.**	Thursday
*States**	**GA**	Georgia	**VT**	Vermont
	KS	Kansas	**OR**	Oregon

* Special two-letter abbreviations for state names are used with zip codes. Both letters are capitalized, and no period is used.

Directions: Write the correct abbreviation for each underlined word.

1. <u>Doctor</u> John Harrison

____

2. Monday, <u>August</u> 4

____

3. 156 Peachtree <u>Street</u>

____

4. Thomas Marx <u>Junior</u>

____

5. Aunt Bessie in <u>Oregon</u>

____

6. Old South <u>Company</u>

____

7. 6258 Western <u>Avenue</u>

____

8. <u>Mister</u> Thomas Graham

____

9. (<u>married woman</u>) Crow

____

10. <u>Post Office</u> Box 47825

____

Commas in a Series

Use **commas (,)** to separate words in a series of three or more items. Use *and* before the last word in a series. **Note**: Do *not* place a comma after the last word in a series.

Example: Jamie, Chuck, **and** David played baseball.
Pam danced, sang, **and** acted in the play.

Directions: Place commas where needed in the following sentences.

1. Maria planted pansies roses and daisies in her garden.

2. On Tuesday Wednesday and Thursday it rained.

3. Philadelphia Chicago and Atlanta have orchestras.

4. The immigrants came from Poland Germany and Italy.

5. Yellowstone Glacier and Yosemite are national parks.

6. Please bring a notebook paper and pencil to class.

7. Skateboards rollerblades and bicycles were on sale.

8. The school colors were red gold and yellow.

9. Math science and social studies are my favorite subjects.

10. Mother bought eggs milk cheese and bread at the store.

11. Lisa Bobby and Andrea may go to lunch first.

Introductory Words and Phrases

A **comma** (,) follows an introductory word or phrase to separate it from the rest of the sentence. Use a comma after *yes, no, well*, and order words (*first, second, next, finally*).

Example: Yes**,** I like chocolate cake and ice cream.
After the play**,** we went for pizza.

Use a **comma** to set off the name of a person being addressed.

Example: Jeremy**,** show us the photos of your new bicycle.

Directions: Add commas where needed below.

1. First read the directions before beginning.

2. Next study the examples given.

3. Harriett have you read the directions?

4. Yes she told the teacher she had read the directions.

5. Before your dinner wash your hands.

6. Robert have you washed your hands?

7. No I need to change my shoes first.

8. Well there will be no dinner until you do.

9. Finally we can eat our dinner.

Dates, Greetings, and Closings

A **comma** (,) is placed between the date of the month and the year. A comma is also used after the year within a sentence.

Example: On August 25, 1995, Andre Tucker was born.

A **comma** (,) is placed after the greeting in a friendly letter and after the closing in any letter.

Example: Dear Uncle Henry,
Sincerely yours,

Directions: Using commas correctly, punctuate the following. Remember all the rules of punctuation.

1. Ferdinand Magellan left Spain on September 20 1519.

2. His ships reached Rio de Janeiro on December 13 1519.

3. On October 21 1520 the ships entered a passage that was later called the Strait of Magellan.

4. November 28 1520

Dear King Charles

Sincerely yours
Ferdinand Magellan

5. Magellan was killed on April 27 1521 in a fight with natives.

A **quotation** is the exact words that someone says. It always begins and ends with quotation marks (" ").

Example: Thomas asked, "Are you going to the video store?"

The end marks and commas are placed **inside** the quotation marks.

Example: Agnes replied, "I am going to the video store."

Some quotations may be divided. If the divided quotation is one sentence, separate the speaker's name from the quotation using **commas** (,). If the quotation is two sentences, use a period after the name. Then, capitalize the first word of the second sentence.

Example: "May I go with you," asked Agnes, "or do you want me to ride with Thomas?"

Directions: Rewrite the following sentences on a separate piece of paper. Use end marks and quotation marks wherever needed.

1. Marcia remarked Have you read your science lesson

2. I read the science lesson last night answered Vickie

3. Are you going to the musical this Saturday asked Ebony

4. Are we going bowling asked Chad or are we going skating

5. Yes, we are going bowling Friday responded Adam

Capitalization & Punctuation Review

Directions: First, read each choice carefully. Then, circle the answer that shows the correct punctuation.

1. Caribou are large, wild animals

A. . B. , C. ? D. !

2. A. People use reindeer for food, clothing and shelter,
B. People use reindeer for food clothing and shelter.
C. People use reindeer for food, clothing, and shelter.

3. Did you know that there are Caribou in North America

A. . B. , C. ? D. !

4. A. September 30, 2004
B. September, 30 2004
C. September, 30, 2004

Directions: Circle the answer that shows the correct capitalization.

5. A. Andrew and Melissa rode the school bus.
B. andrew and Melissa rode the school bus.
C. Andrew and melissa rode the school bus.
D. Andrew and Melissa rode the School Bus.

6. A. valentine's Day is February 14.
B. Valentine's day is february 14.
C. Valentine's Day is February 14.
D. Valentine's Day is february 14.

7. A. Dr. anderson and Mr. Johnson played golf today.
B. dr. Anderson and Mr. johnson played golf today.
C. Dr. Anderson and mr. johnson played Golf today.
D. Dr. Anderson and Mr. Johnson played golf today.

To, Two, and *Too*

The words ***to***, ***two***, and ***too*** sound exactly alike, but they are spelled differently and have different meanings. Often, clues in a sentence can help you decide which word to use.

Words	Definitions	Examples
to	in the direction of	Al walked **to** the shop.
two	the number (2)	My cat has **two** kittens.
too	also more than enough	Bob played ball, **too**. Amy danced **too** long.

Directions: Complete each sentence with *to*, *two*, or *too*.

1. Our family owns _____ computers.

2. The Johnson family has computers, ______.

3. There are _____ broken bicycles on the playground.

4. Michael and Jennifer went _____ the toy store.

5. Coach Thomas made us run _____ laps around the field.

6. Please take this mail _____ the next door neighbor.

7. Charles purchased _____ videos last night.

8. I went ____ the store to purchase _____ videos, _____.

9. The math test was not ____ hard for me.

Their, There, and *They're*

The words ***their***, ***there***, and ***they're*** sound alike but have different spellings and meanings. Often clues in the sentence will help you decide which word to use.

Words	Definitions	Examples
their	belonging to them	**Their** car is brand new.
there	at or in that place	My dog is lying **there**.
they're	contraction for the words ***they are***	**They're** coming to the birthday party tonight.

Directions: Fill in the blank with one of the following words: *their*, *there*, or *they're*.

1. ______ is a birthday party for Jessica on Saturday.
2. My best friend and I are going ________.
3. ________ going to play games and skate at the party.
4. Jessica told me that ________ would be ten girls ________.
5. ________ house will be decorated with yellow balloons and pink streamers.
6. ________ Jessica's two favorite colors.
7. ________ will be pizza, chips, ice cream, and cake to eat.
8. Monica and Louise said that ________ presents will be special.

Synonyms

Words that have the same or almost the same meaning are called **synonyms**. You can use your thesaurus to look up synonyms.

Example:

small	little	tiny
big	large	huge
fast	quick	speedy
happy	glad	cheerful
view	see	observe

Directions: Write a synonym for each underlined word.

1. Did you see how speedy the cat was?

2. The tiny bug crawled across the driveway.

3. My large dog barked at the squirrels.

4. Noah was happy to see his grandparents.

5. Did you observe the new student in the cafeteria?

6. That big flower pot was broken during the night.

7. My teacher is always glad to see us in the morning.

p67 – transparency only

Antonyms

Words that have opposite meanings are called **antonyms**. To show how places, things, and people are different, use antonyms.

Example:

big	little
up	down
in	out
top	bottom
friend	enemy
pretty	ugly

Directions: Write an antonym for each underlined word.

1. My sister Mary Alice is too <u>big</u> to ride the roller coaster.

2. Please go <u>down</u> the stairs to find your suitcase.

3. Angela patted the pony's <u>ugly</u> coat.

4. My <u>enemy</u> and I have known each other for seven years.

5. Place this box on the <u>top</u> shelf of the closet.

6. John, take this trash <u>in</u> to the garbage can.

Writing a Friendly Letter

When you write to someone you know, it is called a **friendly letter**. A friendly letter is written to tell about something that you have seen or done. It can also be written to ask how a friend or relative is doing.

A friendly letter contains the following:

1. The **heading** gives the writer's address and the date.
2. The **greeting** begins with *Dear* and the name of the person who receives the letter. Begin each word with a capital letter, and place a comma after the person's name.
3. The **body** is the main part of the letter.
4. The **closing** is the ending of the letter. Some closings are *Your friend*, *Sincerely*, *Yours truly*, and *Love*.
5. The **signature** is the writer's name.

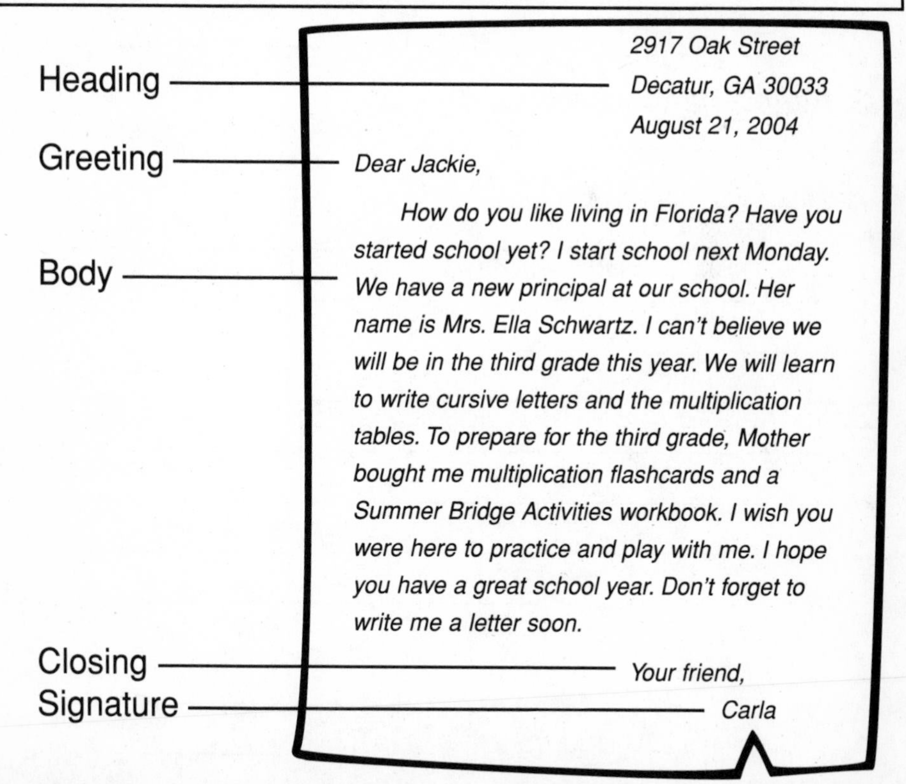

2917 Oak Street
Decatur, GA 30033
August 21, 2004

Dear Jackie,

How do you like living in Florida? Have you started school yet? I start school next Monday. We have a new principal at our school. Her name is Mrs. Ella Schwartz. I can't believe we will be in the third grade this year. We will learn to write cursive letters and the multiplication tables. To prepare for the third grade, Mother bought me multiplication flashcards and a Summer Bridge Activities workbook. I wish you were here to practice and play with me. I hope you have a great school year. Don't forget to write me a letter soon.

Your friend,
Carla

Writing a Friendly Letter

How to Write a Friendly Letter:

1. **Select** someone you want to write to.
2. **Prepare** a list of things you want to say in your letter.
3. **Write the letter**. As you write the letter, include the five parts: the heading, the greeting, the body, the closing, and the signature.
4. **Proofread** your letter. You may want to use a dictionary to check your spelling.
5. **Write the final copy** of your letter. Be sure that it is neat.
6. Finally, **address the envelope** and place a stamp on it. Then, mail your letter.

Directions: Write a friendly letter on the lines below.

Goofy Grammar 1 & 2

Directions: This is fun to do with friends; however, you can do this on your own, too. Before reading the stories on pages 72 and 73, fill in the blanks below with a word for each category. Use the words you have chosen to fill in the blanks in the story. Read the story aloud with your words.

Story 1

noun __________
adjective __________
plural noun __________
plural noun __________
adjective __________
plural noun __________
plural noun __________
verb __________
verb __________
noun __________
verb __________
noun __________
plural noun __________
noun __________
verb __________
adverb __________
verb __________
verb __________

Story 2

adjective __________
verb __________
verb __________
verb __________
verb __________
proper noun __________
adjective __________
adjective __________
adverb __________
noun __________
adjective __________
verb __________
noun __________
verb __________
verb __________

Goofy Grammar 1

The elephant is the largest living land ________ (noun). There are two ________ (adjective) kinds of elephants. One is the African elephant, which has large ________ (plural noun), and both the male and female have ________ (plural noun). The other is the Indian elephant, which has ________ (adjective) ears, and only the male has ________ (plural noun).

An elephant's trunk does not have ________ (plural noun), but it does have muscles. It is used to ________ (verb) up grass and leaves and ________ (verb) them to the elephant's ________ (noun). The trunk is also used to bring water to the elephants mouth or to ________ (verb) it on the elephant's ________ (noun). Other uses for the trunk include making trumpet calls, pulling down ________ (plural noun), and smelling the ________ (noun).

Even though elephants weigh a great deal, they ________ (verb) almost ________ (adverb). They ________ (verb) at a speed of almost 4 miles an hour and can ________ (verb) at almost 25 miles an hour.

Goofy Grammar 2

Three ________ goldfish ________ in the little pond. All
adjective / verb

day long they would ________ and ________. Sometimes
verb / verb

they would even ________ into the air.
verb

The oldest one was named __________, and he would be
proper noun

one year old on Friday. This goldfish was kind of __________
adjective

and __________. This meant that the other goldfish acted
adjective

________ towards him. He didn't care too much because he
adverb

knew that they looked to him for __________.
noun

The middle goldfish was named Fred. He was very

__________ to the others. Fred wanted to be just like the old-
adjective

est goldfish. He followed him around the pond and

__________ just like the older one.
verb

Alden was the youngest goldfish. He wanted to be a

________. Because of that he would __________ all day long.
noun / verb

These three goldfish were best of friends. They continued to

live in the pond and ________ for their whole lives.
verb

Page 1

1. raccoons, animals, night
2. North America, kinds, raccoons
3. raccoon, pounds
4. raccoon, rings, tail, mask, face
5. Raccoons, areas, woods, water
6. foods, frogs, fish, acorns
7. food, night, dens, day
8. Raccoons, areas, dens, log, stump, tree
9. Colonists, raccoons, pelts, caps, overcoats, robes

Page 2

1. Mice, rodents, teeth
2. snout, body
3. Harvest mice, areas
4. grasshopper mouse, plains, deserts
5. insects, scorpions
6. pygmy mouse, mouse, world
7. Field mice, plants, insects
8. mice, burrows, logs
9. house mouse, type
10. White mice, pets

Page 3

Part I July, Atlanta, Eiffel Tower, Civil War, Jessica, Drew School

Part II

1. Dr. Goodroe
2. Jeffrey, John, Ann, Dr. Goodroe
3. Peachtree Street, Atlanta, Georgia
4. December **5.** Grand Canyon
6. Uncle Jonathan, San Diego Zoo

Page 4

1. hats **2.** shoes **3.** coats
4. boxes **5.** trunks **6.** sisters
7. dresses **8.** friends **9.** boys
10. beaches **11.** brushes **12.** lunches
13. clocks **14.** birds **15.** stores
16. passes **17.** students **18.** chairs
19. floors **20.** ducks **21.** churches
22. foxes **23.** boats **24.** drums

Page 5

1. class's teacher **2.** dog's tail
3. tree's leaves **4.** athlete's shoes
5. student's books **6.** boy's uncle
7. teacher's papers **8.** woman's dresses
9. ballplayer's bat **10.** band's leader

Page 6

1. babies' **2.** students' **3.** watches'
4. grandparents' **5.** brothers' **6.** aunts'
7. trees' **8.** dogs' **9.** boys'

Page 7

Mammoth Cave National Park

Mammoth Cave is part of the world's longest known cave system. It is surrounded by Mammoth Cave National Park. The park is located in central Kentucky. The Green and Nolin Rivers flow through the park. This national park was started in 1941.

Mammoth Cave is sometimes called one of the wonders of the Western Hemisphere. The cave is located on a ridge made mainly of limestone. There are 12 miles of corridors through which visitors can be guided. The cave has five levels. The lowest level is 360 feet below the surface of the earth. There are many rocks in the cave which have interesting colors and shapes.

Several lakes, rivers, and waterfalls can be found in the cave. The largest river, Echo River, varies in width from 20 to 60 feet and 5 to 25 feet in depth. Strange, eyeless fish live in Echo River. They are about three inches long and are colorless. Beetles and crayfish are two other blind creatures that live in Mammoth Cave.

Page 8

1. we **2.** I **3.** You, It **4.** They, us
5. He, she, them **6.** They
7. It, He, or She **8.** he **9.** We

Page 9

1. she, her **2.** him, he **3.** them, they
4. her, it **5.** it **6.** she, her
7. they, them **8.** it **9.** she, he, her
10. they, them **11.** He **12.** You
13. she **14.** We **15.** it **16.** them **17.** him

Page 10

1. I **2.** It **3.** We **4.** They
5. You **6.** They **7.** We
8. He, She, or It **9.** She

Page 11

1. them **2.** me **3.** him **4.** her
5. them **6.** me **7.** us **8.** him

Answer Pages

Page 12
1. My **2.** your **3.** our **4.** his **5.** Their
6. your **7.** my **8.** his **9.** mine **10.** Her

Page 13
1. you'd **2.** he's **3.** it's

Page 14
1. We are **2.** I will **3.** she will
4. he is **5.** He had **6.** it is
7. They will **8.** I am **9.** she is
10. You will **11.** I will **12.** they are
13. We had **14.** You had

Page 15
1. C **2.** A **3.** B **4.** D **5.** A **6.** C
7. D **8.** B **9.** A **10.** B **11.** A

Page 16
1. pulled **2.** built **3.** carried **4.** helped
5. protected **6.** called **7.** looked
8. had **9.** carried **10.** crossed

Page 17
1. perform **2.** weld, drill, paint
3. produce, wrap **4.** assemble
5. performs **6.** control
7. search **8.** explore **9.** equip

Page 18
1. is **2.** are **3.** is **4.** was, is
5. are **6.** were **7.** are

Page 19
1. use **2.** make **3.** spins **4.** swings
5. traps **6.** have **7.** use

Page 20
1. traveled **2.** arrived **3.** roamed
4. allowed **5.** stopped **6.** studied
7. received

Page 21
1. will write **2.** will study **3.** will sing
4. will enjoy **5.** will plan **6.** past
7. past **8.** present **9.** future **10.** future

Page 22
1. has **2.** have **3.** had, had **4.** has
5. have **6.** had **7.** have

Page 23
1. ran **2.** saw **3.** come **4.** went
5. seen **6.** ran **7.** go **8.** come

Page 24
1. eat **2.** sang **3.** given **4.** took
5. begin **6.** grown **7.** taken **8.** grew
9. begun

Page 25
1. can't **2.** haven't **3.** couldn't
4. weren't **5.** doesn't **6.** shouldn't
7. could not **8.** does not **9.** have not
10. cannot

Page 26
List: run, pulled, carried, searched, are, used, trapped, stops, spins, sang, enjoying, learned, saw, came, wouldn't, began, helped, is, wasn't
1. played **2.** carried **3.** seen
4. stops **5.** watched **6.** began
7. have **8.** wasn't

Page 27
1. B **2.** C **3.** B **4.** C
5. C **6.** A **7.** D **8.** C

Page 28

[1]p	[2]o	s	s	e	s	s	i	v	e	[3]p	r	o	n	o	u	n	
	b									a							
	j									s						[4]f	
	e			[5]s	u	b	j	e	c	t	p	r	o	n	o	u	n
	c									t						t	
	t				[6]a					e						u	
	p				[7]c	o	m	m	o	n	n	o	u	n		r	
	r				t					s						e	
	o				i					e						t	
	n				o											e	
	o		[8]c	o	n	t	r	a	c	t	i	o	n			n	
	u				v											s	
	n				e											e	
				[9]p	r	o	p	e	r	n	o	u	n				
					b												

Page 29
1. The, the, largest
2. Most, big, the
3. Rural, large
4. Most, one, two-room, stone, abode, clay, tile
5. poor, the, main
6. the, juicy, wheat, a
7. the, most, popular
8. the, many, beautiful
9. Many, colorful

Page 30

1. Most, gas **2.** This **3.** Some **4.** hot-air
5. paper **6.** Each **7.** British

Page 31

1. Many **2.** three **3.** seven
4. several **5.** thirty
6–10 Answers will vary.

Page 32

Stalactite

A beautiful stone formation found in some limestone caves is a/the stalactite. Stalactites hang from the walls or roofs of the caves. Some resemble draperies or straws with a hole through the center, but most look like an icicle.

Most stalactites are formed by water dripping in a/the cave. When the water drips, it leaves behind a small amount of minerals. These minerals build up very slowly and form stalactites. Examples of a stalactite can be found in the Carlsbad Caverns in New Mexico.

Page 33 (Answers will vary.)

Page 34

1. bigger **2.** longest **3.** longest
4. smaller **5.** largest **6.** cutest
7. colder

Page 35

1. happily **2.** carefully **3.** quickly
4. gracefully **5.** Suddenly **6.** neatly
7. hungrily **8.** Slowly **9.** gently
10. noisily

Page 36

1. always **2.** Yesterday **3.** often
4. today **5.** Now **6.** when
7. how **8.** how **9.** when

Page 37

1. outside **2.** far **3.** There **4.** ahead
5–7 Answers will vary.

Page 38 (Answers will vary.)

Rhinoceros

The rhinoceros had two horns. She always used them for digging and fighting. The mother rhinoceros walked carefully in the grass looking for food. The rhinoceros eats mostly bulbs, grass, and other plants. She was extremely protective of her baby. The baby wandered around trying to investigate his surroundings. Often, the mother nudged the baby back into the tall grass for protection.

Yesterday, the mother had to fight enemies to protect her baby. She used her horns, which are made mainly of the same protein found in hair. The rhinoceros always depends on its sense of smell because it has poor eyesight.

Now, the baby depends on his mother for food. Later, as the baby grows, he learns to find food on his own. This baby is about two or two-and-a-half years old. Soon he will leave his mother to live on his own.

Page 39 (Answers will vary.)

Page 40

1. C **2.** A **3.** C **4.** A
5. B **6.** C **7.** C **8.** A

Page 41

1. ADV **2.** ADJ **3.** ADV
4. ADJ **5.** ADV **6.** ADV
7. ADV **8.** ADJ **9.** ADJ

Page 42

1. adjective **2.** verb **3.** adjective
4. adverb **5.** noun **6.** adjective
7. verb **8.** noun **9.** verb **10.** adjective

Page 43

1. Three dogs ran quickly.
2. A mockingbird flew fast.
3. The cow mooed loudly.
4. Seven children raced quickly.
5. Thirteen puppies played happily.
6. The musician played beautifully.
7. A butterfly landed gently.
8. Twenty-five students talked noisily.

Page 44

1. D **2.** A **3.** D **4.** B
5. C **6.** D **7.** A **8.** D
9. C **10.** B **11.** D **12.** A
13. A **14.** A **15.** C **16.** A

Page 45

1. S **2.** NS **3.** NS **4.** S **5.** NS
6. NS **7.** S **8.** S **9.** NS

Page 46

1. S **2.** Q **3.** Q **4.** S

5. My dog Coco loves to sleep and eat.
6. What do you think Coco's favorite foods are?
7. Would you believe she eats vegetables and fruits?
8. Coco loves to chase squirrels and cats from the yard.

Page 47 (Answers may vary.)

1. Jupiter is covered by clouds, which are organized into bands.
2. It has an unusual feature called the Great Red Spot.
3. A dark ring of dust was discovered by the *Voyager* spacecraft.
4. The planet Jupiter has at least sixteen moons.

Page 48

1. C **2.** C/E **3.** E **4.** C/E **5.** E/C
6. C **7.** C **8.** E/C **9.** C **10.** C

Page 49 (Answers will vary.)

Page 50

1. Easter Island
2. It
3. The early islanders
4. Most of the people
5. More than 600 statues
6. The islanders
7. They
8. Huge, red stone cylinders

Page 51

1. cuts through northwestern Arizona
2. varies in width from less than 1 mile to 18 miles
3. flows through the canyon
4. formed the canyon over millions of years
5. date back two billion years
6. has about 120 kinds of animals
7. thrive on the canyon's rim
8. have lived in the Grand Canyon

Page 52

1. NS **2.** S **3.** NS **4.** S
5. Q **6.** C **7.** S **8.** E or C

9. The Empire State Building cost $41 million.
10. The limestone and steel building was not original.
11. The original owners depended on sightseers to pay the building's taxes.

Page 53

Considered by many to be America's finest author, Jack London was born on Market Street in San Francisco. His name at birth was John Griffith Chaney. He was the son of William Chaney, an astrologer and journalist. His father deserted Jack's mother, Flora, before Jack was born. Later, Flora married John London, a Civil War veteran. Much of Jack's youth was spent in Oakland, California, on the waterfront.

Jack had little formal schooling. He attended school only through the eighth grade, although he was an avid reader. In later years, Jack returned to high school in Oakland and graduated.

He became the best selling, highest paid, and most popular American author of his time. His most notable book, *The Call of the Wild*, is considered an all-time classic.

Page 54

(in any order) Monday, Oak Street, Katherine, President Bush, Mr. Thomas, Piedmont Park, South Dakota, Robert

1. Saturn **2.** Jupiter, Saturn
3. Saturn, Titan **4.** Saturn, *Voyager*

Page 55

1. May – Memorial Day, Mother's Day
2. October – Columbus Day, Halloween
3. February – Valentine's Day
4. December – Christmas, Hanukkah
5. January – New Year's Day, Martin Luther King Day
6. Monday, Wednesday, Thursday, Saturday, Sunday

Page 56

1. Tues. **2.** Oct. **3.** Mr. David Park
4. *The Wizard of Oz* **5.** *Treasure Island*
6. "Over the Rainbow"
7. Rev. Mark Bowling
8. Miss Wendy Clark

Answer Pages

Page 57

1. My friend Jonathan hiked through the Grand Canyon.
2. Sarah is a nurse at Northside Hospital on Johnson Road.
3. When we were in Chicago, we swam in Lake Michigan.
4. In Paris, there is a famous church called Notre Dame.
5. Last year, our class visited the Louvre, a famous art museum.

Page 58

1. Be sure to take water and food with you.
2. Wear warm clothes while mountain climbing.
3. How many students are mountain climbing today?
4. Are you afraid to go mountain climbing?
5. You will see beautiful scenery while mountain climbing.
6. Wow, what a breathtaking view that is!
7. Is it time to eat lunch?
8. Look at the wild flowers growing in the distance.

Page 59

1. Dr. **2.** Aug. **3.** St. **4.** Jr. **5.** OR
6. Co. **7.** Ave. **8.** Mr. **9.** Mrs. **10.** P.O.

Page 60

1. pansies, roses, and daisies
2. Tuesday, Wednesday, and Thursday
3. Philadelphia, Chicago, and Atlanta
4. Poland, Germany, and Italy
5. Yellowstone, Glacier, and Yosemite
6. notebook, paper, and pencil
7. Skateboards, rollerblades, and bicycles
8. red, gold, and yellow
9. Math, science, and social studies
10. eggs, milk, cheese, and bread
11. Lisa, Bobby, and Andrea

Page 61

1. First, **2.** Next, **3.** Harriett,
4. Yes, **5.** dinner, **6.** Robert,
7. No, **8.** Well, **9.** Finally,

Page 62

1. September 20, 1519
2. December 13, 1519
3. On October 21, 1520,
4. November 28, 1520
Dear King Charles,
Sincerely yours,
5. April 27, 1521,

Page 63

1. Marcia remarked, "Have you read your science lesson?"
2. "I read the science lesson last night," answered Vickie.
3. "Are you gong to the musical this Saturday?" asked Ebony.
4. "Are we going bowling," asked Chad, "or are we going skating?"
5. "Yes, we are going bowling Friday," responded Adam.

Page 64

1. A **2.** C **3.** C **4.** A
5. A **6.** C **7.** D

Page 65

1. two **2.** too **3.** two
4. to **5.** two **6.** to
7. two **8.** to, two, too **9.** too

Page 66

1. There **2.** there **3.** They're
4. there, there **5.** Their **6.** They're
7. There **8.** their

Page 67 (Answers may vary.)

1. Did you see how fast the cat was?
2. The little bug crawled across the driveway.
3. My huge dog barked at the squirrels.
4. Noah was glad to see his grandparents.
5. Did you see the new student in the cafeteria?
6. That large flower pot was broken during the night.
7. My teacher is always happy to see us in the morning.

Page 68

1. My sister Mary Alice is too little to ride the roller coaster.
2. Please go up the stairs to find your suitcase.
3. Angela patted the pony's pretty coat.
4. My friend and I have known each other for seven years.
5. Place this box on the bottom shelf of the closet.
6. John, take this trash out to the garbage can.